A DORLING KINDERSLEY BOOK

Note to parents

My New School is designed to introduce young children to the idea of starting school. It aims to dispel any fears they may have about meeting new teachers and classmates. The story will also help a younger sibling understand what an older brother or sister does at school every day. Each scene introduces young children to some of the experiences that they will encounter in their first days at school, such as shared reading and playing, cooperating, and creative activities. By looking at this photographic story together, and using each picture as a starting point for discussion, you will help your child to realize that starting school is a rich and rewarding experience that offers an exciting, new independence.

Editor Stella Love
Art Editor Yaël Freudmann
U.S. Editors B. Alison Weir and Lara Tankel
Production Marguerite Fenn
Managing Art Editor Chris Legee
Managing Editor Jane Yorke

Photography by Susanna Price
Illustrations by Julie Carpenter
Models Hayley Georgiou, Max Lee,
Kim Ng, and Zanepierre Antoine

First American Edition, 1992
10 9 8 7 6 5 4 3 2 1

Published in the United States by
Dorling Kindersley, Inc., 232 Madison Avenue
New York, New York 10016

ISBN 1-56458-116-0

Library of Congress Catalog Card Number 92-52812

Color reproduction by Colourscan
Printed in Italy by New Interlitho

STARTING
OUT

My New School

Written by
Harriet Hains

DORLING KINDERSLEY, INC.

NEW YORK

Starting school

Today is Lucy's first day of school.
She feels nervous as she waves
good-bye to her mommy.
"Hello, Lucy," says Ms. Brown
kindly. "I am your new teacher.
This is Max.
It's his first day, too."

Lucy and Max hang up their coats.
They both feel quiet and shy.

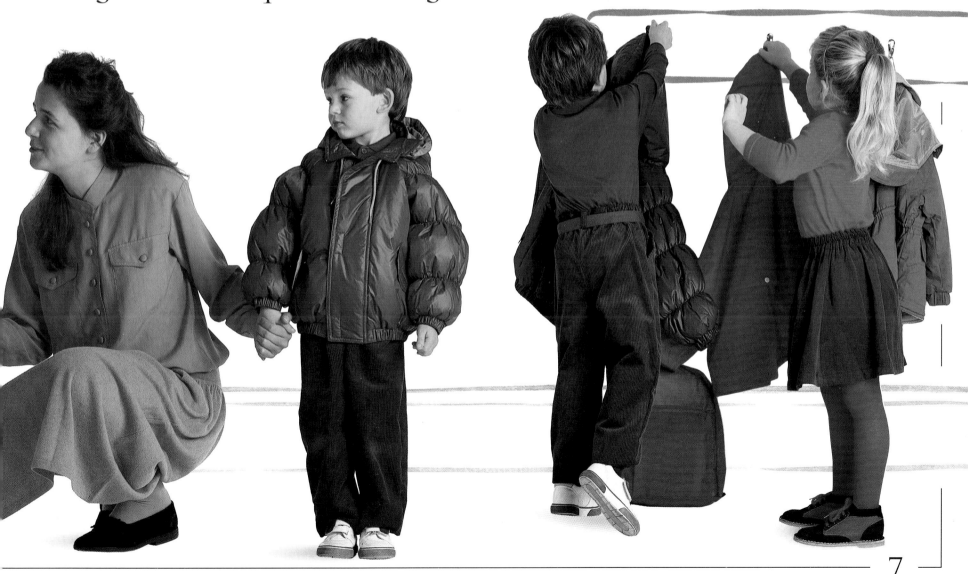

In the classroom

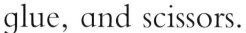

"Would you like to make a mask
with the others?" asks Ms. Brown.
Lucy and Max fetch some crayons,
glue, and scissors.

They sit down with Paul and Kim.
"My mask is bright green," says Paul.
Lucy carefully writes her name on
the back of her mask.

Playing together

"I'm a scary monster!" roars Kim.
"You look funny," giggles Lucy.

Next, Lucy and Kim
put on their smocks.
Soon they are busy
making shapes
in the sand.

In the playground

"Look at me!" calls Lucy
to her new friends.
She spins the hula-hoop
around and around.

"Come and play with us," calls Paul.
"Catch, Max!" says Kim.

Painting

After play, it is time for painting.
"I think I will put some stars in the sky,"
says Max.

"Let's hang our pictures on the wall," says Paul. Lucy tapes up her picture first, then Paul's.

Building blocks

Ms. Brown shows Lucy and
Max the building blocks.
"I want to make a tower," says Max.
"I'll make one, too," says Lucy,
not feeling shy at all.

"Look, this one is the tallest," she says.
Lucy puts one more block on top.
"Oh, no! It's wobbling!" cries Max.

In the book corner

"Time to read a story,"
says Ms. Brown.
The class sits down together.
Everyone looks at the pictures.
"What is happening here?"
asks Ms. Brown.

Story time is over.
"You may all choose a
book to read at home,"
says Ms. Brown.
Lucy can't make up her mind.
"I like all the books!" she says.

Time to go

It is time to go home.
Lucy and her new friends
put on their coats and
pack their bags.
"Bye-bye," says Lucy,
"See you tomorrow."
  She runs off happily
    to meet her mommy.